Original title:
Roots Beneath the Soil

Copyright © 2025 Creative Arts Management OÜ
All rights reserved.

Author: Ronan Whitfield
ISBN HARDBACK: 978-1-80581-920-2
ISBN PAPERBACK: 978-1-80581-447-4
ISBN EBOOK: 978-1-80581-920-2

Secrets in the Shadows

In the garden, whispers play,
Mice dance, while the cat's away.
Worms tell tales of underground flair,
While ants host shows with snacks to share.

Beneath the surface, laughter thrives,
Dirt and giggles, nature's jive.
A gopher burps, a squirrel grins,
In this world, everyone wins.

The Latticework of Life

Beneath our feet, a tangled maze,
Insects buzz, and mischief plays.
A beetle spins like it's on a stage,
While fungi write their life's page.

They plot and scheme, a grand ballet,
A tiny world, in disarray.
With every squirm, there's laughter loud,
A funny place, that soil crowd.

Harmony in the Darkness

In the gloom, where shadows creep,
Wiggly things with secrets to keep.
They hum a tune of pure delight,
Making mischief from day to night.

The moles sing songs of daring feats,
While bugs waltz to nature's beats.
A symphony of chuckles played,
In dark corners, fun's displayed.

Portraits of the Unseen

In the depths, a world concealed,
Sassy roots and laughter revealed.
A snail poses, puts on a show,
While mushrooms dance with a groovy flow.

With each twist, a comic act,
Nature's jesters in a pact.
They paint the soil with fun and cheer,
In their gallery, we all draw near.

The Silent Network

Underneath the grass so green,
Worms in coats of dirt are seen.
Chattering secrets, they conspire,
To play hide and seek, they never tire.

Moles with shades and sneaky grins,
Throwing parties where chaos begins.
The dance of roots, a twirl and slide,
Fungi joining in, with joy they bide.

Where the Earth Breathes

Down below where whispers dwell,
Tiny creatures weave their spell.
Ants on stilts in a marching line,
Hoping to find the perfect vine.

A snail with swagger, slow and loud,
Claims the title, 'Most Laid Back' proud.
While beetles giggle at their race,
Do they know it's just a silly chase?

Echoes from the Deep

In caverns deep, a giggle stirs,
A chorus of chuckles, all from furs.
Rats wear hats made from fallen leaves,
Proud of their style, oh what a tease!

Skunks with colognes, thinking they're suave,
Turning the woodlands into a rave.
Mice tap dance on a mushroom top,
In this strange party, no one wants to stop!

Embrace of the Subterranean

Down in the burrow, laughter rings,
A squirrel plays with the funniest things.
A cloud of dirt, a tumble here,
As rabbits hop, with cheer they steer.

The gophers gossip, they can't be beat,
Trading tales of their underground meet.
In this silly realm of underground play,
You never know what might happen today!

Nature's Underbelly

Beneath the ground, a wiggly dance,
   Earthworms wiggle in a trance.
They gossip of the night's big feast,
While dancing on a mushroom least.

Mice wear hats made of fine grass,
Holding parties where toasts amass.
   Each seedling sings a silly tune,
As bugs tap dance beneath the moon.

The Gracious Embrace of the Depths

Down where the roots curl and twist,
The toadstools plot, they can't resist.
They laugh at flowers up above,
Who think they're hot in sunny love.

Mole whispers jokes that bring a cheer,
To critters hiding down in here.
Laughter bubbles in the damp,
Where shadows find their afternoon camp.

Nourishment from the Hidden

Up in the light, the veggies tease,
'We're brighter than the trees!
But down here we know the juicy truth,
The dirt-dwelling life's a laugh-filled booth!

Beetles brag of shiny shells,
While snails compose their slimy spells.
Root vegetables get giggle fits,
As they play tag with little bits.

Beneath the Mulch, Stories Stir

Under mulchy blankets thick and brown,
Secrets whisper, never frown.
A cricket tells of gopher fights,
While ants rehearse their dance delights.

From the compost, tales emerge,
Of carrots plotting a great dirge.
They prance around with radish flair,
In underground, a comedy fair!

Lifting the Veil of the Underground

In the dark where critters dwell,
They throw a party, oh, what the hell!
Worms in tuxedos dance with glee,
Raccoons invite the ants for tea.

Banana peels become the floor,
While fungi croon; they're never a bore.
'Who's got the snacks?' the moles all shout,
'Just one more bite, then we'll head out!'

Beneath the Surface, Life Thrives

In morning mist, the potatoes grin,
Swaying with laughter, they start to spin.
Beetles bust moves; it's a real ball,
Chard gives a wink, 'Let's show them all!'

'We're deep down but never alone,'
Said the carrots, adjusting their cone.
'What's the weather like? We're too deep!'
'It's fab, my friends, let's take a leap!'

The Power of Unseen Bonds

A secret crew in the damp and dark,
Spin tales of mischief, leave a mark.
'You think we're quiet? Just wait and see!'
Said the mushrooms, sharing their spree.

Together we stand, though out of sight,
Chatting and plotting till the morn's light.
'The snacks are gone, who ate the last?'
'Hands up! Don't look at me, I'm aghast!'

Deep Connections in Stillness

In silence thick, the laughter rings,
Mice in capes discuss their flings.
Crickets chirp a jazzy tune,
While dirt-dwellers start to swoon.

'Let's start a band!' cried one brave bug,
The ant replied, 'I'll give a hug!'
Together they jam, the roots shake hands,
Who knew the earth could have such bands?

Unseen Connections

In the dark they wrestle, those cheeky kin,
Sneaking and creeping, digging in.
They giggle and chuckle beneath the ground,
Trading whispers with worms all around.

Their meetings are secret, their laughter is sly,
When humans walk over, they just wave hi.
On a quest for the best dirt, they plot and they scheme,
With the wiggle of soil, they live in a dream.

The Network of Nourishment

They send each other snacks like a foodie spree,
A banquet of minerals, oh dear me!
Sending out pizzas with roots made of cheese,
The underground diners dine at their ease.

A tomato and carrot play peek-a-boo,
Discussing the flavor of morning dew.
With a side of earthworms, they share a toast,
To the underground life that they love the most.

Veins of Existence

It's a party beneath with no need for light,
Where radishes waltz with parsnips all night.
They dance in the dark, it's all quite absurd,
A silly little shuffle without a word.

With tiny confetti from dirt and from sand,
They giggle and jiggle, it's all quite unplanned.
But if you ask the mushrooms, they'd say it's the best,
A soily celebration, just let them rest.

The Language of the Ground

In tongues made of tread and marvelous muck,
They whisper sweet nothings, a little bit of luck.
With tutus of turf and hats made of clay,
They throw up their roots and dance all day.

They gossip about rain and the sun's golden rays,
And share hilarious tales of the very best days.
Their jokes might be corny, a bit of a mess,
But in their rich humor, they surely impress.

Tunnels of Time

Through winding paths they waddle and weave,
The secrets of dirt, you wouldn't believe!
A worm in a tux, and a bug in a hat,
Throwing a party, where's the party at?

They dance with the beetles, boogie with glee,
Digging up treasures; a shoe or a key.
They gossip of gardens, tell tales of the day,
In tunnels so funny, come join in the play!

The Cradle of Growth

Down where the seeds go to sleep and to snore,
An acorn has dreams of being much more.
The plants on the rise, they stomp and they shout,
'We're coming for sunshine, watch out, look out!'

With wiggles and giggles, they start their parade,
An onion's confessions, a carrot, afraid.
'Where's our dear sunlight?' they march in a line,
Chasing their dreams, growing funny and fine!

Beneath the Canopy of Leaves

Under a carpet of a leaf-laden quilt,
The antics of critters jauntily built.
A squirrel with acorns, a dance on the ground,
Rodentia rave, oh what joys have they found!

Clovers are laughing, a dance in a twist,
While mushrooms play maracas, you get the gist.
With giggles and wiggles, they spring in delight,
Beneath all the green, there's a party tonight!

The Silent Symphony of Soil

A chorus of clumps all singing in tune,
The earth's very own squatters' cartoon.
With fungi as conductors, they're loud and quite bold,
Reciting the tales of the dirt and the cold.

A pebble in percussion, the grubs are the strings,
A mallet of mushrooms, oh the joy that it brings.
With laughter aloft in the dark and the damp,
The symphony plays, with the soil as the champ!

The Substantial Veil

Beneath the ground, the secrets play,
Where worms are kings in their own way.
They wiggle, squirm, and twist with grace,
In a soil ball, they form a race.

Beets and carrots do the tango,
As turnips hum a cheeky jango.
The radish teeters, oh, so bold,
While potatoes gossip tales of old.

And every root seems quite aloof,
While underground they play goof-proof.
They whisper tales of wiggly fun,
In their earthy kingdom, never done.

A Dance of Hidden Threads

Underneath the grassy patch,
Unseen, the critters start to hatch.
They cha-cha in the moonlight glow,
While moles keep time with feet below.

The daisies cheer them on with glee,
As creeping vines swing with such spree.
The daisies roll in laughter, too,
At the antics of their leafy crew.

The dance of flora in disguise,
Invisible to our human eyes.
Yet underfoot, they twist and spin,
In a merry world where laughs begin.

The Spread of Stillness

In the quiet, things do roam,
For all the plants have made a home.
While daisies dream of sunny beams,
Their pals below plot silly schemes.

The clovers giggle, feeling nice,
As roots are frequently precise.
They stretch and yawn, with flair and fright,
Causing mischief in the night.

Old oak trees tell tales of woe,
Of grumpy weeds who steal the show.
They puff their leaves with all their might,
While fungi wear a cap for light.

Depths of Interconnection

Underneath, where all is hush,
The plants hold hands in friendly crush.
They trade old secrets and some dirt,
While teasing snails dress up in skirts.

The secret life of roots and more,
Like toddlers hiding by the door.
Their tiny roots play peek-a-boo,
With all the critters passing through.

In soil's embrace, they find their spree,
While copper beetles sip sweet tea.
Giggling fungi throw confetti,
As they recruit new pals—come, get ready!

The Language of Earth's Embrace

In whispers soft, the ground does speak,
Little critters trend, oh so unique.
They plot and scheme beneath our feet,
Planning a dance, quite a funny feat.

With wiggles, shakes, and tiny grins,
The soil's secrets hide their whims.
A council of roots, so bold and spry,
Gossiping tales as time slips by.

Moles gossip about the worms' new trends,
While beetles share who is making amends.
In this hidden world, full of cheer,
Who knew dirt could tickle your ear?

So next time you think of silent ground,
Remember the laughs that swirl around.
Beneath your steps, a comedy flows,
A party of critters that nobody knows.

Fertile Whispers in the Caverns

Beneath the trees where shadows dwell,
Giggles spill from a mushroom shell.
In earthy halls, they twist and twine,
Their pranks and jokes are quite divine.

The fungi boast of their fungal flair,
While roots compete for the best soap air.
Sipping on dew from morning's cup,
A merry band, never giving up.

There's a rumor of a rockstar snail,
Who plays the ukulele with a big, long tail.
And nightly, the beetles throw a bash,
With boogie beats but a not-so-fast dash.

So lend an ear to the caverns wide,
Where laughter frolics and worms abide.
With each rumble, a punchline may drop,
In this underground circus, they never stop.

Ancestral Threads in the Dark

In darkened realms where laughter thrives,
Old tales of glory take joyous dives.
A family of tubers, tangled and proud,
Share secrets and jokes, beneath the crowd.

Granny's old wisdom, in twists and knots,
Cousins play pranks, tying all the pots.
While uncles brag of their longest stretch,
A legacy found in each silly sketch.

Sister roots gossip about last night's brawl,
As curious ants make a call to all.
They cheerfully argue who shimmied best,
In the muddy depths, it's a comical fest.

So when you tread on that fertile ground,
Remember the laughter swirling around.
In the dark, ancestral threads spin and dance,
Bringing humor to each circumstance.

Cascading Connectivity

In the tangled web of green delight,
Laughter flows fast, taking flight.
The petals gossip about the leaves,
While the ground chuckles, pulling sleeves.

A funny handshake of sprouting vines,
Tickling the toes of curious pines.
Each twist and turn a hearty jest,
Giggling mosses put humor to the test.

Rabbits trade tales of the grass's tricks,
While knowing the humor in their flicks.
And when the rain adds a slippery twist,
Oh, how the roots laugh, they can't resist!

So dance with the quirks of nature's play,
Where mirth and glee rule the day.
For in this web, each giggle's free,
Just ask the wiggly worm, he'll agree!

The Lattice of Life Below

In the dark where critters scheme,
They hold a dance, a wiggly dream.
With tiny hats and tiny shoes,
They plot the pranks that they will choose.

A gopher's giggle, a mole's delight,
They trade tall tales, all through the night.
The earthworms twist with laughter grand,
While ants tap dance, a merry band.

The beetles boast of travels wide,
While rooty pals provide the ride.
"Oh look, a shoe! Let's take a peek!"
But alas, it's a trap, they squeal and squeak.

So underfoot, the laughter flows,
In secret rooms where mischief grows.
A wilder world we cannot see,
Where all of life holds a jubilee.

Streams of Existence Underfoot

There's a stream where puddles share,
And with a splish, they dance with flair.
A fish in need of a bubble bath,
Squeaks through gravel, starts a laugh.

The tangles twist, with pebbles rolled,
A party here that's never old.
The snails are DJing, spinning tracks,
As slugs dance forth in shiny slacks.

A worm with dreams of goldfish fame,
Tries karaoke, but can't sing a name.
The chorus croaks, the crickets play,
Laughing loudly at the worm's cabaret.

Beneath our feet, a splashy show,
Where creatures thrive and giggles flow.
So if you hear a gurgling cheer,
It's life below, full of good cheer.

Tunneling Through Time

Digging deep with tiny tools,
The earthlings play like joyful fools.
A mole constructs a mansion grand,
While pushing dirt with cheerful hands.

Each tunnel leads to a new surprise,
A party where the beetle flies.
They dine on roots, time truly flies,
With cactus juice and bug-sized pies.

A time machine? Oh, what a bore!
They'd rather dig up snacks galore.
"Let's unearth the ancient peas!"
They munch and chuckle, "What ta tease!"

So when you tread upon the ground,
Know beneath, the laughter's found.
Creatures wriggle, playing today,
In their odd, hilarious way.

Dialogues of Silence

In silence whispers still abound,
Where secrets linger, seldom found.
The fungi gossip in the night,
While seedlings giggle, feeling bright.

Behind the scenes, the mushrooms chat,
"Did you hear what the tree did? That!"
They hold a meeting, sans the light,
With shady jokes that feel just right.

The pebbles roll their eyes in jest,
"What's up with roots? They think they're best!"
While twigs all nod in perfect time,
They share their tales, fun and sublime.

So next time when you stroll above,
Remember life that's full of love.
They chat in silence, find delight,
In all the quirks that take to flight.

Echoes of the Ancient Ground

In the quiet where whispers dwell,
Worms giggle, playing hide and swell.
Old tales of dirt, they all recite,
As ants march on with their tiny plight.

Beneath the crust, a party's rife,
Where moles debate the joys of life.
A radish wears a leafy crown,
While tubers dance beneath the town.

Trees drop secrets in leafy foam,
While beetles claim the underground dome.
The wind can't reach this joyous crew,
But they throw dirt pies just for you.

So if you think life's just above,
Listen close to those below with love.
A world of chuckles, jokes and more,
Where laughter sprouts from every floor.

Threads of Life Intertwined

In the soil's embrace, the threads do twist,
With fungi laughing, they can't resist.
Twirl around in a silly waltz,
Beneath the ground, there are no faults.

Rabbits share their funny lore,
While crickets tap at the earthen door.
A dandelion starts to dance,
As moles join in a silly prance.

The earthworms wiggle, it's quite a sight,
Telling jokes deep into the night.
While roots play twister, tangling tight,
They all agree that they're a fright.

So heed their laughter, join the fun,
For in this ground, there's no need to run.
Each giggle underfoot is fine,
A comical bond where they all shine.

The Pulse of the Underneath

Beneath our feet, the pulse beats strong,
With shovels tapping a hidden song.
The carrots hum, the potatoes cheer,
As life below grows crystal clear.

A dance-off starts with worms in line,
Judged by crickets sipping on brine.
The radishes shout "We're full of zest!"
While turnips boast of who looks best.

Ants hold meetings, plotting schemes,
While dreaming of their chocolate dreams.
Grass roots whisper, "Don't start a fight,"
But even they can't hide delight.

So when you tread upon the ground,
Remember joy is waiting, profound.
With every step, a jig, a shiver,
Beneath the surface, life's a river.

Shadows Cradling Growth

In dimly lit nooks where silliness blooms,
Shadows tickle the earth with their plumes.
The broccoli giggles, the peas take a bow,
As beetles burst forth for a raucous wow.

Underneath, the dance floor shakes,
With clovers laughing, each twist it makes.
The daffodils wear hats of delight,
While spiders spin stories late at night.

Who knew the ground could host such fun?
With whispering seeds, and honey to run.
A rock band of roots plays with glee,
Performing for critters, entertainingly free.

So next time you see a flower sway,
Remember the shadows have come out to play.
In the depths below, joy takes its toll,
While laughter rises from the heart of the knoll.

Buried Stories

In the garden, secrets thrive,
Underneath, the rumors dive.
Worms whisper tales of silly strife,
Of garden gnomes and tiny life.

Old potatoes share a grin,
While carrots giggle from within.
They throw a party underground,
Where laughter's lost but joy is found.

A beet boasts of its color bold,
While radishes reveal the mold.
Potting soil's a cozy chair,
For tales that spin through fragrant air.

So dig a little, take a peek,
You never know what it might speak.
In hidden nooks, the funny waits,
With tales of dirt and garden mates.

The Echo of Forgotten Lives

What's that sound beneath my feet?
A chorus of the things we meet.
Ghostly giggles, echoes play,
From critters living day by day.

A mole sings songs of ancient fights,
While crickets dance on endless nights.
With every bump, a tale unfolds,
Of mischief that the darkness holds.

Forgotten roots turn to pranks,
As trees exchange their leafy thanks.
"Did you hear the one about the thistle?"
"Yeah, it sure knows how to whistle!"

Underneath, the laughter swells,
In every nook, a story dwells.
So kick the dirt and lend an ear,
To echoes of the whimsy near.

Kinship in the Dark

Buried buddies make their plans,
Plotting laughs with squishy hands.
Wiggly worms in a dance unite,
In the cozy, loamy night.

A tuber tells a joke so bright,
Causing mushrooms to take flight.
"Why did the fungus cross the lane?
To simmer in the veggie chain!"

They share their dreams of reaching fame,
In the big, wide world, it's all the same.
Together in the dark, they thrive,
A veggie team, so very alive!

What's life without a little jest?
In the earth, they feel so blessed.
So let's all dig and find our kin,
In the subterranean din!

The Veiled Embrace

Underneath, they hold a ball,
With soil-caked selves, they have a ball.
Peas in shoes, and corn in hats,
Dancing 'neath the friendly chats.

"Who wore it better?" asks the sprout,
While onions laugh, both round about.
"Don't trip on worms!" a cabbage calls,
As laughter echoes through the halls.

A radish spins, its leaves a swirl,
And carrots cheer, "Let's watch it twirl!"
Each tiny root shares secret dreams,
In silken dark, where laughter gleams.

So pull a chair and join the fun,
For life below has just begun.
In stitched-up darkness, friendships bloom,
A veiled embrace, where joy finds room.

Whispered Secrets of the Earth

Under the ground where the gophers dance,
Worms tell jokes at their wild romance.
Grubs and bugs share a laugh or two,
In their underground, hullabaloo!

Rocks might grumble, roots might sway,
While mushrooms giggle, enjoying the play.
The soil's a stage for the critters' show,
With punchlines hidden where no one can go!

Ants wear hats, so snug and neat,
Swapping stories with a tiny fleet.
With twinkling eyes they plot and scheme,
In their busy world, it's a funny dream!

Oh, the chuckles echoed far and wide,
In the underground, where secrets slide.
Each little creature has a part to play,
In the comedy club of the earthy ballet!

Veins of the Hidden World

Under the grass, a tale unfolds,
Where the laughter of fungi never gets old.
Tiny trees in a line, they giggle and cheer,
As the beetles roll barrels, bringing the beer!

A chipmunk complains that his acorns are fat,
While a mole in his glasses looks quite like a cat.
Squirrels are jesters, flipping their tails,
While the ants plan their trickster trails!

Earthworms do squats, they're in for a thrill,
Flexing their muscles, they're all about skill.
A gopher sings songs, a delightful refrain,
While the roots just chuckle, it's all in the game!

Rabbits wink down from a bush up high,
Their laughter resounding beneath the bright sky.
In this secret world, funny antics abound,
With the mirth of the underground always spellbound!

Silent Stories in the Dark

In the shadows where critters all skulk,
The jokes hit harder than a rolling bulk.
Raccoons tell tales, all giggles and grins,
While the snakes share secrets with their slithery spins!

Beetles on bikes race in the gloom,
While a worm does the worm, busting a groove.
Squishy and silly, they frolic about,
In a world where laughter is always in clout!

A porcupine juggles with pinecone balls,
While the hedgehogs gather to cheer in the halls.
The night blooms with humor, a carnival's spark,
As the critters all gather, creating a lark!

The moon is a spotlight, casting its glow,
On the giggling secrets that only they know.
In their shadowy realm, life's funny and sweet,
Every root whispers tales that tickle the feet!

The Tapestry Below

Beneath our feet, a lively fair,
With mushrooms laughing, currying flair.
Squirrels in costume strut about,
Hosting a ball with a raucous shout!

Dirt has its own peculiar scribes,
Who pen down jokes full of fun vibes.
Ants design hats for the highest ants,
While the tiny toads join in the prance!

In the midnight hour, the raccoons conspire,
Sharing their pranks, while the roots admire.
The party's electric, with no need for light,
As giggles erupt into the starry night!

The tapestry weaves a tale so grand,
Of critters and giggles on this playful land.
Each little brownie under the ground,
Knows in this world, laughter does abound!

The Depths Hidden Away

In the dark where secrets creep,
Worms and bugs hold secrets deep.
They giggle low, they wiggle wide,
In their underground homes they bide.

Potatoes dress in muddy coats,
Throwing parties with dirtier notes.
Carrots dance in their leafy hats,
Waving to all the tippy-tap rats.

Dandelions whisper tales of woe,
Of gardeners who pull and throw.
But deep in their cozy beds,
They laugh at all the garden threads.

Oh, to be a seed in the ground,
With a buffet of muck all around.
A tickle of rain, a splash of sun,
From here, we know we've just begun!

Lifelines in Darkness

Beneath where the sun forgets to shine,
Cousin mushrooms sip on their wine.
They toast to the ferns, ancient and wise,
As they peek through the soil with tiny eyes.

The thump of a shovel starts a dance,
'Oh no!' scream the bugs, 'this is our chance!'
But the more they panic, the more they trip,
On earthworms leading a wild hip-hop skip.

Each root creeps under with a silly grin,
Making mischief where no one's been.
They tickle the toes of the giant trees,
Saying, "Join us for lunch, we'll bring the cheese!"

In the gloom, when the shadows play,
The funny friends have their own cabaret.
With giggles and hops, they steal the show,
When the moon peeks in with a bright hello!

The Underworld Symphony

In the dark is a rhythmic beat,
A symphony of worms on tiny feet.
They tap and dance on the damp, cool ground,
With no one to hear, their joy's unbound.

Moles conduct with their noses in air,
As critters join in without a care.
The acorns drop like beats on the floor,
While the ants march by, calling for more.

The soil hums a jovial tone,
A chorus of laughter, never alone.
Each creature brings their own special part,
In this concert of life, full of heart.

So if you can't hear the music above,
Just listen for giggles, the sound of love.
In the darkness, where joy can grow,
A secret party thrives down below!

Paths Made of Memory

Underneath, where shadows play,
The memories linger without decay.
Old leaves whisper tales of yore,
Of sunshine and storms that knocked at the door.

In tunnels of time, laughter remained,
As critters dug paths, uncontained.
A light-hearted race to the old oak tree,
Where stories are shared, carefree and free.

The dancing roots sketch out a map,
'This is where we had our best nap!'
With wildflowers painting the tales they spread,
It's all in the fun when you're lightly fed.

So here we gather, in muck and mirth,
Join the underground for all it's worth.
Their playful stories, forever unfold,
In lines of laughter, both young and old.

Tales of Subterranean Growth

Deep down where the moles like to play,
Curly mustaches have much to say.
Worms wear tuxedos for the soil dance,
Throw in some radishes, give them a chance.

The carrots claim they're the best of the bunch,
While beets are plotting a foolproof punch.
Each tuber whispers a secret or two,
But the onions just cry, it's all they can do!

Sassy potatoes with skins full of cheer,
Have a root party whenever they hear.
The radishes giggle, the garlic takes flight,
Underneath all this, there's pure delight!

In this underground world, mischief does thrive,
Where all of our veggies just want to survive.
A leafy affair, they dance and they sway,
Making each day feel like a bright cabaret!

The Depths of Resilience

Down where the sun's rays can't peek through,
A potato dreams of being part of a stew.
With a wink and a nod, it forms quite a clique,
While telling the turnips, "Let's play a trick!"

The beets roll their eyes, tried and true,
Saying, "We're sweeter, who cares what you do?"
But the parsnips just chuckle, flipping their greens,
"Don't mind the spuds, they're all in their jeans!"

A tussle erupts as cabbages spin,
Brussels sprouts giggle, it's all a win-win.
Each root, full of spirit and humor galore,
Creates comical tales of what's in store.

So here in the dark, where laughter's the sound,
Life thrives in layers, this fun underground.
Beneath the hard surface, the jests never cease,
In a whimsical world, they find their peace!

Webs of Ancient Kinship

In dusty hallways where history creeps,
The whispers of fungi are secrets to keep.
With roots intertwined in some cosmic ballet,
They joke about sunlight and who'll get the ray!

A radish tells stories of days gone by,
While vining green peas just giggle and sigh.
"Last harvest!" they chuckle, "We're quite the crew,
Staying together, it's what veggies do!"

The gentle potato got caught in a vine,
Its buddies all chuckled, "Oh look at him shine!
He thinks he's pasta, but what a mistake,
Just dig him back up; he's best when we bake!"

In this underground world, love and jest grow,
Mixing with humor, a colorful show.
They cheer for each other, sprouting their dreams,
Life in the dark is as bright as it seems!

Sinews of the Earth

Where the dirt squishes, and laughter is grand,
Carrots are planning a dance-off so planned.
"The best in their class," they all start to boast,
But radishes tease, "We're the ones with the most!"

Potatoes are digging, and roots start to sing,
Chanting of harvest and all that it brings.
In cobwebs of wonder, they twist and they twirl,
While the turnips just giggle, "Let's give it a whirl!"

The onions hold secrets, sharing their blend,
While the peas play tag, like sweet little friends.
In tunnels they roam, with laughter and glee,
Finding new ways to be joyous and free.

So here in the depths, where quirkiness reigns,
Mischief and joy course through all their veins.
These sinews of laughter beneath cover whole,
Bring mirth to the dark, that's their common goal!

The Strength Found in Shadows

In dark corners they wiggle and squirm,
Finding light in their underground term.
With a giggle and grunt, they come alive,
These little jokers in earth's big hive.

They tug at the weeds, oh what a sight,
Dancing around, giving weeds a fright.
Must be a party, with snacks down below,
Playing hide and seek in the soil's warm glow.

Cradled by the Unseen

They whisper secrets in silence so deep,
While up above, the flowers peep.
In tangled tales of mischief and cheer,
They giggle softly, oh dear, oh dear!

With a tickle here and a nudge or two,
They plan a little prank, it's nothing new.
Knocking on mushrooms, what a fun game!
Wishing the world could just know their name.

The Fertile Depths Sing

Oh, the merry band of earthy delight,
Singing sweet songs in the dead of night.
With voices like crickets, they harmonize,
While the world above just sighs and sighs.

Soil symphonies rise in hidden joy,
A raucous choir, oh boy, oh boy!
They tap dance under the moon's silvery beam,
Living their life like a glorious dream.

Veiled Vitality

Under the surface, there's laughter galore,
Like a raucous party behind a closed door.
They swear they'll pop up just for a glance,
But only if you dare to join their dance.

With a wink and a nod, they pull on a string,
As seedlings above do a little spring fling.
Stealthy and sneaky, they nibble and chew,
The elves of the earth, with a trick or two.

Beneath the Surface

Worms have parties, oh what a sight,
Dancing all day and jiving all night.
With dirt on their shoes and hats askew,
They invite the moles, who bring their own brew.

The gophers gossip, their whispers profound,
Telling tales of the treasure they've found.
They've stashed away snacks from the farmer's stash,
Cushioned by soil, just for a bash.

Laughter erupts from the bug brigade,
As ants pull pranks in their grand charade.
They juggle pebbles with effortless flair,
Creating a circus beneath the rare air.

Foundations of the Ancients

There once was a tree with roots like a maze,
It held the wisdom of ancient days.
Its branches know secrets of things long gone,
While critters debate who can dance on the lawn.

One squirrel claimed it's a wise old sage,
With tales of the past, like a timeless page.
The raccoon laughed and said, 'Oh please!
You're just jealous I'm friends with the bees!

Underneath, a party's brewing wild,
With mushrooms grooving, like a carefree child.
The beetles form bands, with a rhythm so fine,
While ivy joins in, claiming, "This beat's divine!"

Murmurs from the Buried Past

The earth's full of chatter, oh what a ruckus,
With old bones debating, who's really the luckiest?
Rabbits retrace paths that their grandpas made,
While worms tell stories of the times they played.

A ghostly old turf does vaudeville acts,
With props made of pebbles and hilarious facts.
The snails clapped along to the rhythm of roots,
While crickets crooned, in their favorite boots.

The legends linger, making things fun,
With wise old rocks under the sun.
A turtle once whispered, 'Forget about fuss,
Life's just a game, come join in the rush!'

Ties that Bind

Underground donuts are baked by a mole,
His secret ingredient? A roll and a stroll!
A chorus of critters chant, 'Let's dig in fast!'
While munching on treats from the ages past.

The field mice chatter about grand escape,
With capers and plans that are maybe not safe.
A badger's the planner, he's got all the schemes,
While toads run the kitchen, fulfilling their dreams.

So raise a toast with a dandelion drink,
To friends underground who never do blink.
With laughter and antics, life flourishes well,
In this quirky abode, where everyone dwells.

The Quiet Heart of Nature

In the garden, worms dance slow,
They wiggle, twist, and steal the show.
While daisies gossip, petals in bloom,
The radishes dream of world tours, I presume.

The beetroot thinks it's a celebrity,
Strutting roots like a fancy caddy.
Meanwhile, grass just laughs in glee,
Why bother with fame when roots are free?

Forming networks like a tiny chat,
Underground meetings—who's there? A rat!
Giggling moles play hide and seek,
While the daisies sigh, "Oh, we're so chic!"

But if you peek beneath the green,
You'll find the quirks not often seen.
Nature's heart, so deeply funny,
Giggles here are sweet as honey!

Unraveled Threads

In the earth, tales unwind,
A tangle of secrets, sweetly twined.
Old carrots whisper to the peas,
"Why do you smile? It's just a breeze!"

The spinach swears it knows the score,
While turnips plot a play for more.
Potatoes dream of idle fame,
But forget they're just a salad's game.

The radishes wink in shades of red,
Sharing jokes from their cozy bed.
'How do you turnip for a rave?'
'With roots so groovy, we misbehave!'

As earthworms twist with cheeky flair,
They say, "It's dark, but we don't care!"
With every giggle and soil-y jest,
Their tangled lives are simply the best!

The Hidden Tapestry

Under the grass, a party brews,
With mushrooms grooving in colorful hues.
Dandelions sport hats made of dew,
In a world where the soil's the star of the show!

A party of tubers, dancing with glee,
"Who needs sunlight when we can just be?"
Beneath the ground, a hidden spree,
Where each twist and turn is pure jubilee.

The roots sing songs of forgotten glories,
While rocks sneak in with their own stories.
"Why do you stay down here all day?"
"Because these roots have the best cabaret!"

So join the laughter, do take a peek,
At a world where the whispers are not so meek.
A hidden tapestry of life, I say,
Come dance with us, let your soil sway!

Requiem of the Underscape

Here lies the grand tale of the unsung sprout,
A little hero, in echoes, shouts.
With a chuckle, the garlic huddles tight,
It's all about cloves, who needs the light?

The beets throw shade, their humor sly,
"Why can't we be on Netflix? Oh, why?"
The underground's a sitcom, I swear,
Where laughter germinates everywhere.

The squash throw a party, but wait, what's that?
A plucky little onion enters, looking flat!
"Don't cry for me, I'm spiced with zest!"
The dance floor erupts; it's simply the best!

So here in the depths, it's a raucous crowd,
With chuckles and giggles that ring out loud.
The requiem sings of the lives we led,
In this rooty farce, no one's misread!

The Lush Secret World

In the garden below, there's a gnome,
Digging for snacks, all alone.
He shoves his face in a tuber of yams,
Convinced they'll make him a king of the jams.

The worms hold a party, all dressed up in flair,
With soil as their dance floor, they twirl without care.
The ladybugs gossip about the best spots,
While the snails race for gold, with a promise of crocs.

The ants form a band, playing tiny guitars,
Singing songs of the dirt, beneath the stars.
With laughter and cheer, they dance and they play,
In the lush secret world, where odd critters stay.

Currents of the Deep

Beneath the ground, the critters all scheme,
As they plot out escape, like a wacky dream.
The moles are wearing sunglasses, feeling so cool,
While the rabbits all teach them the rules of the pool.

In burrows so snug, the badgers make stew,
Out of acorns and berries—it's quite the hullabaloo!
The hedgehogs roll over, laughing with glee,
As the chipmunks all ponder, 'Is that dinner for me?'

The roaches recite poetry under the light,
And the beetles keep rhythm, feeling just right.
In currents of dark, lives a party unseen,
Where the underground dwellers live life like a dream.

The Forged Bonds

A squirrel named Timmy made friends with a snail,
Who taught him to groove on the slick garden trail.
They'd vibe to the rain and they'd share all their snacks,
Best pals forever, no worries or hacks.

The toads all sang ballads, their voices a thrill,
While the bees brought the honey to sweeten the chill.
With glee in their hearts, they'd gather at dusk,
In mudpie competitions, oh what a robust!

The antics were wild, a real hootenanny,
Playing games with the worms, and sipping on fanny.
In their jolly alliance, they'd laugh till they cried,
In the forged bonds of friendship, they take great pride.

Fertile Foundations

In a kingdom of chaos beneath the green grass,
A family of moles played hopscotch with sass.
They'd race with each other on paths so obscure,
While the hedgehogs cheered, feeling very demure.

With spades for their shovels and hats made of leaves,
They'd dive into tunnels like crafty little thieves.
The spiders spun webs just to catch all the fun,
While the beetles constructed homes—one by one.

They built up their houses with giggles and glee,
Constructing great motifs, as happy as can be.
In fertile foundations, laughter takes flight,
In the depths of the earth, where joy shines so bright.

Echoes of the Unseen

In the park, the grass is green,
But what's hiding? It feels mean!
Tiny critters hold a ball,
Throw it, and they have a ball!

Worms parade in nature's guise,
Dancing under sunny skies!
With a wiggle and a twirl,
They think they're pretty girls!

Ants march in a perfect line,
Forming paths that intertwine.
One gets lost, oh what a mess,
'Where's the party? I must confess!'

Beneath the turf, the fun is real,
The comedy, an earthy deal!
So while we sit above and sigh,
They're joking hard, oh my, oh my!

The Woven Shadows

In shadows cast by towering trees,
Creatures whisper, 'Look at me, please!'
A rabbit winks, a squirrel grins,
'We're the champs of hiding wins!'

Little feet on trails they scurry,
For a snack, they always hurry.
But wait, what's that? A leaf falls down,
'It's a boulder!' One cried, wearing a frown.

In crowded roots where laughter hides,
Fungi giggle, wearing ties.
A mushroom slips, it lands in goo,
'Watch out, fellas! Here comes the stew!'

The critters play, a raucous show,
Underneath where no one goes.
As we stroll above with pride,
They throw a bash we can't abide!

Soil's Silent Embrace

Beneath the earth, a slumbering crew,
With tiny dreams and wiggly view.
A potato puffed, said, 'I'm a star!'
While carrots whisper, 'Don't go far!'

A rock grumbled, 'I'm just a stone,'
'But underground, I hold my throne!'
The mushrooms chuckled, 'Join the fun,
We'll have a party when day is done!'

In tunnels deep, the secrets dwell,
With tales of roots and how they swell.
A gopher cracks a cheesy pun,
'You dig my jokes, or are we done?'

So if you scoff at what's below,
Remember, there's quite a show!
For every laugh we think we know,
Is echoed softly in the flow!

A Tale of Entwined Lives

A carrot talked to a beet,
"You think you're so sweet?"
They giggled in the dark,
Underneath the park.

A tomato joined the chat,
Said, "I'm the king of that!"
But the onion rolled its eyes,
"Let's not get lost in lies."

Together they laid low,
In dirt, they'd steal the show.
With roots all intertwined,
They found fun unconfined.

In shadows they play pranks,
Spilling muck on fancy tanks.
Who knew that muck could spark,
Such laughter in the dark?

The Beneath We Forget

In a world beneath our feet,
Worms dance to a funky beat.
They twirl with glee and laughter,
In their own merry hereafter.

Mossy parties happening fast,
Old leaves tell stories from the past.
"Did you hear the one about the root?"
"Of course, but that's a hoot!"

Rabbits pop down for a peek,
To listen to the gossip they seek.
"Oh, the celery's so dramatic!"
"I swear, it's a real acrobatic!"

So if you roam where you don't see,
Remember the giggling greenery.
Life's rascals, they find joy,
In dirt, their favorite toy.

Life's Secret Chorus

In the dark where giggles grow,
The secret choir puts on a show.
A radish sings, a pepper hums,
To the rhythms of the drums.

Beneath the surface, mischief brews,
With plants donned in vibrant hues.
"Let's serenade the farmer's cow!"
"No way, let's sing 'How Now!'"

The beats electrify the earth,
Bringing laughter, bringing mirth.
Nightly fiestas give a cheer,
For bunnies sneaking near.

So when you hear the soil shake,
Know the fun is not a flake.
For down below, they chortle, dance,
In unity, their lives enhance.

Memory of the Underground

Down below, where secrets throng,
The fungi sing their funky song.
A mushroom twirls, a sprout does leap,
While ants march in a line so deep.

They hold a party, raucous, grand,
In the warm and squishy land.
"Bring snacks!" the grumpy radish said,
"Or I might just lose my head!"

Tales of bugs and nighttime fright,
Make for laughter by moonlight.
In slimy realms where few will roam,
They claim this shadowed home.

So raise a glass of dirt-filled cheer,
To all the critters we hold dear.
For memories beyond the sun,
Are masked in laughter, wild fun!

Bloodlines of the Earth

In the garden, gophers roam,
Digging tunnels, calling home.
Plant a seed, they pull it down,
With a chuckle, wearing frowns.

Worms are dancing, doing jazz,
Underfoot they all amass.
While the daisies sip on dew,
Giggling all the morning through.

Tangled twigs and laughing vines,
Whisper secrets, draw the lines.
With the ants they share a joke,
While the daisies gently poke.

Earth's big family bustles deep,
Counting giggles, keeping sheep.
Moles on Mondays look for cheese,
In the soil, they rule with ease.

A Canvas of the Unnoticed

Underneath, a party brews,
Mice with hats and dapper shoes.
Every root a brush, they paint,
Making art without restraint.

Worms are poets, penning rhyme,
On the clock, they never chime.
Rabbits in their rich attire,
Jumping high as they conspire.

The mushrooms wear a pointy cap,
Dreaming dreams in grassy lap.
Crickets chirp a rap so sweet,
To the snails they move their feet.

Every creature finds its place,
In this underground embrace.
The unseen's joy, let's give a cheer,
For the art that lives down here!

Beneath Our Feet

In the dirt, a world of thrills,
Critters munching on their meals.
Moles are chefs, they bake with flair,
While bugs dance, without a care.

Under rocks, the lizards chat,
Planning parties, how about that?
Ladybugs wear polka dots,
Holding court in muddy spots.

Spiders weave their webby jokes,
Snakes are cracking up in hoax.
While the dew drops form a tear,
Laughter echoes far and near.

Every nook has tales to tell,
Silent giggles weave a spell.
In the muck, let's spread the cheer,
For the fun hidden right down here!

The Silent Abode

In a shush, the critters jive,
Underneath, they're all alive.
A raccoon plays the tambourine,
As the beetles tap their routine.

Crabgrass holds a concert loud,
While the ants form up a crowd.
Each blade of grass, a microphone,
In the soil, they make their throne.

Old roots laugh as they recall,
When the squirrels would almost fall.
Warmth and joy beneath the ground,
In the quiet, fun abounds.

Check the laughter, bright and spry,
Wonders flourish, oh my my!
In this hidden, lively scene,
Nature chuckles, ever keen.

The Shade of Hidden Life

In the ground, where the giggles grow,
Little critters put on a show.
Worms dance under the moon's soft light,
While ants have a party, oh what a sight!

Mice leathered in mist, they play peek-a-boo,
With dandelion cakes, who knew?
They sip on dew drops like fancy wine,
Sneaking crumbs from the picnic line.

Down below, the secrets are spun,
Chatty roots have a ton of fun.
They tell wild tales of the weather above,
And giggle at clouds that fall in love.

Life's a party under the ground,
With all kinds of pals that can't be found.
So lift your feet, and take a glance,
There's more to this world than just happenstance.

The Network of Emily

Emily's cable of connections grows,
With chatterbox roots and tipsy toes.
They swap secrets with mushrooms galore,
And play cards with gophers—Oh, what a score!

One wiggly worm caught in a bind,
Said, "I'm just too popular, oh so unkind!"
The beetles laugh, rolling on the grass,
While the daisies gossip, letting time pass.

Emily thinks of a leaf to wear,
Planning a dress for the underground fair.
A wild costume of clay and moss,
But watch out for the snails—don't be the boss!

The roots bring everyone something to share,
From cranky old frogs to a fleeting hare.
All gather 'round for their laugh-a-thon,
Down in the burrows, the jam goes on!

Comforts in the Dark

In cozy corners where shadows creep,
Little critters snuggle and slowly peep.
A hedgehog reads a novel, out loud,
While a giggly toad forms a curious crowd.

They share stories of wriggly stress,
Of daring escapes and well-placed mess.
With fungi lamps that flicker and glow,
Their night-time chatter puts on a show.

A family of mice with popcorn in tow,
Join in for a movie, cinematic glow.
"How to Dance Like a Dandelion," they cheer,
With fluffy popcorn filling their ear.

The dark is a comfort, a hug from below,
Where mischief flourishes and laughter can flow.
When life gets too bright, they just come alive,
In the cozy embrace where all snooze and thrive.

Sanctum of the Subsoil

Deep down below, there's a sanctuary sweet,
Where guffaws echo and sweet things meet.
A squirrel on drums makes the soil vibrate,
While dandelions rap about a bright fate.

Under cover of earth, the fun begins,
With earthy delights and playful spins.
Grub chefs preparing a feast that's quite grand,
As beetles bring side dishes—oh, isn't life planned!

With laughter that bubbles, like roots in the rain,
They celebrate life, with no hint of pain.
The underground disco spins round and round,
With glowworms grooving, all lost and found.

So next time you tread on the ground overhead,
Just know there's a ruckus going on instead.
In the sanctum of subsoil, it's all a delight,
Where creatures are dancing, hidden from sight!

Secrets of the Hidden Earth

In muddy caverns, critters dwell,
Finding treasures, oh what a smell!
They trade old marbles for shiny stones,
And giggle at jokes in their comfy homes.

With tinfoil hats, they plot and scheme,
While worms hum tunes in a wiggly dream.
Who knew the dirt had such grand design?
To host a party for a mole or a vine!

The ants are cater waiters, zipping around,
Serving up snacks from the underground.
While beetles debate who's the best band,
In this secret world beneath, oh so grand!

And they all know that when humans tread,
There's nothing but chaos; they scurry and flee instead!
Oh, if only they knew what's under their feet,
A raucous parade that could never be beat!

Life In the Silent Depths

Deep in the chatterwood, the gophers plot,
With schemes so absurd, it's hard to keep caught.
They dance like dervishes, diggin' away,
Creating caverns for a nut buffet!

The snails are the DJs, spinning some tunes,
While crickets are joining with hopping festoons.
With a roast of old roots on a leafy plate,
They rave through the night, oh isn't it great?

Beneath the chaos, a wise old toad thinks,
"What if we painted our backs with old inks?"
But the show, oh dear, took a slipp'ry slide,
Now everyone's wearing their friends as a ride!

So laugh with the critters in their silent dismay,
Life below isn't dull; it's just a different play.
Join in the fun, take a dive, don't resist,
In the depths, oh my friend, a wild party exists!

Tendrils of History

In ancient tunnels of time they wriggle,
Past secrets and laughter, their giggles are biggle.
Old histories lie under rocks and twigs,
While mushrooms play music, and garden snakes jig!

The moles tell tall tales of great gopher fights,
Who wore the best costume at the last moonlight nights.
They whisper of treasures all shiny and bright,
That only the brave can find by moonlight!

As crickets recite marvelous myths,
Of the great ancient worm and its legendary zips.
The saga unfolds with each tiny shake,
Echoed through soil with a giggle and quake!

And so they unite to create a great tome,
Of every creature that calls this place home.
With their stories all penned on a leaf of delight,
This history laughs, oh what a fun sight!

Stories from the Dark Below

In the cozy dark where the critters convene,
They tell wild tales of both funny and mean.
Of a tortoise who raced and lost to a snail,
And an ant who claimed he could sing like a whale!

The bats share their gossip, oh how they swoop,
While the beetles all snicker and form a small troop.
Each burrow is filled with stories so rich,
But the earthworms just laugh; doesn't matter a pitch!

There's a mushroom who swears he saw a lost shoe,
And a rabbit who swears that it's pink, not blue.
So, down in the depths, where the universe spins,
All tales intertwine, while the real fun begins!

So raise up your glasses, to the stories they share,
Down in the dark, where there's laughter in air.
For who could imagine such magic, you see,
In the bustling world of fun under glee!

Through the Dark, New Life

In the depths, where the giggles hide,
Some creatures dance while others glide.
They tickle the ground with silly thrills,
Beneath the grass, they pull off their drills.

Twirling worms show off their moves,
While beetles bust out crazy grooves.
A little mole with a top hat's flair,
Sips tea and laughs in the underground lair.

Dirt is their stage, the earth is their friend,
With comedy acts that never quite end.
They throw a party, with no one to judge,
And sing of their secrets, they won't even budge.

Every chuckle sends a ripple around,
A secret society, where joy can be found.
When you think you're alone, just take a peek,
You'll find their stories, forever unique.

The Heartbeat of the Hidden Realm.

In the quiet, where mischief is planned,
Lies a heartbeat, a whimsical band.
With critters and giggles, they make their play,
Singing of joy in their own silly way.

Tiny toes tap in a jaunty dance,
While squirrels wiggle in a nutty trance.
Bugs don party hats, having a blast,
Making moments of mirth that forever last.

What fun it is, in this secretive spot,
To share in the life that is never forgot.
The laughter they summon is truly divine,
In their cozy confines, oh, how they shine!

Tap your feet if you hear the beat,
A whimsical pulse from a world that's sweet.
Beneath the surface, where surprises bloom,
It's a joyful kingdom, free of gloom.

Whispers of the Underground

In the tunnels where the whispers flow,
Lies a gathering of onlookers in a row.
With carrots for drinks and rhymes for cheer,
They toast to the mud and the squishy frontier.

A nervous toad with a pocketful of jokes,
Cracks up the crowd with his warty folks.
"I went to the surface, it's too bright up there,
I tripped on a root and lost all my hair!"

With giggly gophers cheering him on,
Each tale gets taller; from dusk until dawn.
A banquet of bugs on a leafy spread,
Where laughter and chaos delightfully spread.

So if you hear chuckles from below this ground,
Just know it's a party where smiles abound.
Join in their fun, don't hold back your cheer,
For life underneath is always sincere.

Shadows of the Forgotten

In the gloom where the shadows prance,
Creatures are plotting their secret dance.
Not a worry, no hurry, just giggles and glee,
In the underbelly, where no one can see.

A hedgehog who moonlights as a great comedian,
Tells tales of the surface, the oddest ingredients.
With a high-pitched squeak, he takes his bow,
While the audience chortles, they might just allow.

And there's an old snail with a story or two,
Of how he once raced with a fox and a shrew.
"Slow and steady," he laughs with delight,
"In this hidden world, day blends into night."

So dance with the shadows, embrace their plight,
For laughter is found when it's dark out of sight.
In the depths of the earth, where chaos can fester,
Lay the secrets of life, a comedic jester.

www.ingramcontent.com/pod-product-compliance
Lightning Source LLC
Chambersburg PA
CBHW070304120526
44590CB00017B/2555